10 Easy Steps

to Write Your Novel:

The Quick Start Guide to Novel Writing

Main Idea, Character Development,
Outlining, Writing, and Revising

AUTHORPRENEUR PRESS

Kristen James
editor, novelist and author of

Blockbuster Books, Broken Down
The Novel Map Based on Bestsellers

101 Questions to Improve Your Novel

Authorpreneur: Making Steady Income from Ebook
Royalties

www.writerkristenjames.com

www.amazon.com/author/kristenjames

Kristen James has over thirty published works which have hit the top 100 in Kindle in the US, UK, and Canada. A few of her fiction titles include *Point Hope, More Than Memories,* and *All In My Head*.

www.writerkristenjames.com – novels, nonfiction, editing, speaking, and blog

Table of Contents

Introduction

Stories are the fabric of human of existence. It's how we share our culture and history, how we teach, how we remember, and how we connect. I bet we all have special memories of family stories we heard as children, and memories of someone we love reading to us. We have books that impacted our lives and stay with us. Do you remember the first "big" book you read? Mine was *The Secret Garden.* I got it by accident really, as I'd been reading much shorter chapter books. I had to read it twice, and I can still recall the sense of wonder I felt when I understood it and got lost in the story. It's no wonder that we treasure novels, and that some of us have a burning desire to write one.

I began writing in the fourth grade and decided to be an author. For me, that didn't mean just dreaming about it. I read all the time, began writing stories, subscribed to Writer's Digest, and started my collection of writing books. (Well, my mom might have paid for my WD subscription...) Sometime during seventh grade, I finished my first novel and called my best friend, shaking, to read her the last page. I imagine everyone feels that giddy upon completing their first novel length work, regardless of age! The feeling doesn't go away either—each novel is a journey, learning experience and milestone.

I'm always curious and learning about new things, and my passion for fiction expanded into other kinds of writing and publishing. In 2005, I began freelancing as a ghostwriter and editor while still writing my own books, and I created a full time job around writing and publishing. I've lost count of how many book projects I've worked on either as the author, ghostwriter or editor. Those projects have spanned many different genres, giving me a wide angle view of storytelling.

As a freelancer, I've ghostwritten many nonfiction and business books, and that taught me how to write tightly, use easy to understand language and break information down into usable steps. So of course, as a novelist and writer, I had to start penning my own writing and authorship books. *Authorpreneur*, for instance, is based on my experience as an Indie author. The idea for *Blockbuster Books, Broken Down* hit me when I noticed a few similarities in some of the current bestsellers. When I get a new insight, I want to share with others!

That's where this book comes in. I'm sure you're asking yourself, are there really "ten *easy* steps to write a novel?" Well, I can show you about the *easiest* way to plan and write a novel, but of course writing 50,000 or 65,000 plus words takes some time and effort. That said, using a guide like this can save you countless steps, deleting and rewriting.

I've had times when I got inspired, wrote a novel and truly enjoyed the process. The story flowed like magic. It was like the story already existed, and it was simply waiting for me to write it. But I know it wasn't magic—it happened because I got a spark, developed it, and understood novel structure and how to write compelling characters.

It's my hope that this guide will benefit beginning writers and more experienced ones, so I'm including some items that might sound easy or obvious if you're familiar with the process. That's a good sign! And if everything is new to you, don't worry about it. Just take it one step at a time.

Step 1: Develop your Idea

I start my novel projects by creating a new folder on my desktop where I can store a document for the manuscript, outline, character sheets, notes on writing, cut scenes, and inspirational photos. It keeps it all in one place. You might even start a document for this guide where you can record notes and do the exercises. Many writers prefer to work in Scrivener, which keeps everything in one place too. Other writers might even do all of this work on notepaper. Whatever works best for you, go for it. I've always worked in Word, but I tried Scrivener because so many writers raved about it, and then I went back to Word. I've found a way to mark my scenes and create an outline in Word the way others do in Scrivener, and I'll share that later on.

When I get a new idea, I mull it over for a while and develop it mentally as much as I can, and then I write a working summary. At the end of that, I include any ideas for the plot and characters so I can see my options.

Your first file might summarize the entire story if you're lucky enough to see that much, or it might be the initial conflict. Whatever you have, write it down so you can work with it. First focus on what excites you about the idea, then think about what happens, the conflicts, and how the story might change and evolve. Write down ideas at this stage, and we'll look at how to develop them and put it all together in the following steps.

What about a title?

Coming up with a title can be fun. Or it can be like getting your teeth pulled. I had an easy time creating some of the titles for my novels—they just came to me while writing the story. With others, I struggled through the writing process to find a fitting and catchy title. In the end, I'm very happy with most of them.

At this stage in the game, it's not something to stress over. I start writing down title ideas at the beginning of my novel file so I can work with a list.

Shorter titles usually work better. (In general. There are exceptions to everything.) Smooth or catchy titles work well too. If you find yourself explaining a title, it might be too long or confusing. The title doesn't have to describe the entire story at all, so it helps to remember your title is actually a marketing tool. Think about titles of bestselling books and how short they are, like *The Notebook* by Nicholas Sparks or *Winter Garden* by Kristin Hannah. The title doesn't mean a whole lot either until you've read the book.

For my romances, I came up with fun phrases like *A Cowboy for Christmas* and *More Than Memories.* I have a family drama (married romance) set on the Oregon Coast, and I named it *Point Hope.* To me, that hints at the coast setting and it captures the theme of the novel.

If you get a title idea that just feels right, go with it. I'd still have a list and test it with other people, but I normally feel it when I arrive at the right title for a book.

Developing "Sparks"

I often get an initial spark that I change and develop. One such idea came to me as a tiny scene, almost like a commercial or short dream. A man was leaving his wife for good, and when he stepped out of the front door, he found an abandoned baby.

I usually have no idea where these "sparks" come from, but they often get my mind racing with possibilities. I took the abandoned baby idea and changed it. I didn't think it would actually work to have the baby appear on the doorstep. Instead, a family member died, leaving an orphaned baby girl. This became my novel *Point Hope*.

These sparks can come from anywhere. I've read that Nicholas Sparks based his first hugely successful novel *The Notebook* on his wife's parents. Steffenie Meyer had a dream that inspired *Twilight*. Sometimes a spark comes from an article in the newspaper, a story you overhear, or several things coming together in your mind. Attending literary events and talking to other authors will give you insight into how they find and develop ideas.

Several elements converged into a story for me when I watched snowboarding in the 2014 Winter Olympics. The snowboarders were so different from people I knew. An idea sparked later on as I drove in the country on a sunny day. I was looking out at the green hills when it hit. What would happen if one of those out-going, free spirited snowboarders dated a quiet and reserved college student? No, wait, what if he somehow fell right into her head?

I have no idea how I made the leap from a snowboarder romance to a voice in a girl's head, but I got so excited that I went straight home and started writing. It turned into my novel *All in my Head*.

If you ever get a spark that takes over, go with it! Write while the idea is hot and burning in your mind.

Questions to Consider

1. What's your initial spark? Does it raise questions and make you picture the story?

2. What do you see about your main character? (Or characters?)

3. What most excites you about this idea, plot, and/or characters?

4. If your idea was sparked by something in your life, a real person or story, can you explore that further? You might not use all the real facts, but it can help you explore your emotions and more possible developments for the story.

You won't use all ideas and sparks you get. I've had some that would make great novels, but I'm not excited enough to write them. I just wasn't the writer for that type of story or idea. Other times, the idea isn't strong enough for a full novel.

Sometimes you'll get an idea but won't know what to do with it or where to take it. For about two years, I had this spark of an idea but it didn't feel like enough for a novel. It was almost like a bad dream: A woman wakes up in a hospital and finds a loving husband doting over her, but she doesn't know him. She does have her memory, but both the doctors and the husband act like she has amnesia. The idea raised all kinds of questions. Why did they want her there? Were they lying to her? Was she crazy? Was this a mystery and she was in danger?

That's where it sat for a long time, but something clicked when I realized the obvious, that I'm a romance writer. Suddenly, I knew the husband would be good looking...and dangerous somehow. She'd be attracted to him even while she couldn't trust him.

As I developed the story, I actually gave Megan amnesia, but she had glimpses of her life. What little she did remember didn't match up with what her husband Eli told her. She didn't have any family or friends to turn to, and she was worried she had actually lost it. She couldn't trust herself either, so she was forced to stay with Eli.

Do you see how you can take an idea and run with it, coming up with all kinds of potential conflicts, twists, and even the characters at this point?

My idea became my novel *Stranger in my Bed*, which I classify as romantic suspense for the purpose of Kindle categories. It could fall under a romantic psychological thriller too. If you know what genre you're writing in, it'll give you some guidelines. If you don't know what genre your idea falls under, don't sweat it too much. I've met many writers with a work in progress or even a finished novel, and they still weren't sure what genre it fit into. That usually meant they were looking at all the different aspects and not considering the main one or two. If your idea isn't a mystery, thriller, horror, romance, women's fiction, then it might be general fiction. For now, let's work on developing your novel.

A Solid Foundation

So you have a starting point: a spark or full idea, possibly the plot and maybe the characters. Novels are long, complex projects so it's easy to get caught up in all the details and suddenly see your novel as a giant mountain. I'll guide you through the process in this book, but first let's go through a quick overview. One way to tackle the process is to figure out the big things first and build a solid foundation.

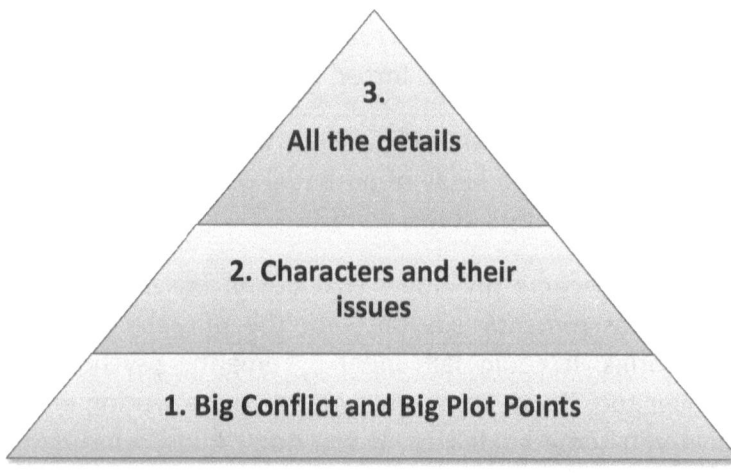

Start with the big conflicts and any big events. This is the idea stage, so you don't have to outline everything—just sketch out what happens. (This often evolves as you plan the novel in more detail.)

I'd like to share a secret with you. The underlying skeleton or foundation is the key to a successful novel. That's the big idea part that grabs readers' attention. You can edit and revise the heck out of a novel, and even spend years on that part, but you might be frosting a rotten cake. I don't say this to scare you, but to encourage you to give this phase the time it deserves. Make sure your big conflicts work. Check that your idea is fresh in some way. Tweak and play with the big elements. Alternatively, consider if your idea is strong enough. Sometimes I get a spark or idea and spend a day thinking it over only to realize it's not that exciting. I might even get to the point of writing it down and then see that it's not much on paper. The good news is, if you build a great foundation, it makes writing the novel so much easier. (And if the writing part is always a struggle, take a look at your foundation to see if you've gone astray from the story or if you might need to rework the foundation.)

Characters and their issues - Next add in your characters and their issues, and by that I mean their "backstory" that will affect the plot. Don't create characters in a vacuum. Instead develop characters that serve your story. If you have a good central conflict (the solid foundation we just talked about) adding the right characters will bring your idea to life, and it'll feel like magic.

As a fun exercise, picture your hero as a pool of gasoline. (Weird, I know, but go with me for a minute.) This person is complex and has inner dissidence—things that just don't jive together but your hero can't fix them yet. This person is propelled through life by hidden pain, past experiences, deep desires, and goals. Then along comes a match named PLOT. This match blows everything all to hell, throwing your character into the most traumatic experience of their life, forcing them to adapt, change and overcome. Your plot should force your hero to face those inner demons or find something to fight for.

Finally add in all the fun details – Now it's time to look at setting, events, character jobs, relationships, and things that you can change without rewriting the entire novel. You don't have to worry about these quite yet, but keep them in mind.

Developing Your Idea Exercises

#1. Take popular novels and try to write a one liner. Describe the two main characters (or one in some cases) and what they're up against.

#2. Brainstorm your main idea and play "what if" to expand it. Can you make your main conflict bigger, affect more people, or worse for the main characters?

Take a page (from a notebook or in Word) and free write about your idea to see where it goes. Start with the initial idea and develop it step by step. This gives you material to work with for the following questions.

Test Your Idea: Turn to your friends and family that are writers or readers, and tell them a quick summary of your book. (Maybe an expanded one liner.) Do they ask questions? That's a very good sign. It means your idea sparks their curiosity and they want to know more.

Step 2: Develop Your Conflict

Do you really know your main conflict?

Let's say you tell a friend you're writing a book, and naturally that friend asks, "So what's it about?"

Can you tell them? I don't mean where and when it's set, or what inspired you to write it, although that's important too. I mean, can you explain your novel in a succulent and short description that describes **what happens?** Even better, can you describe the main point or purpose of your novel, as in **what happens that forces someone to change?** What's the big conflict? What's really at stake?

Look back at the summary you wrote down. Does it include conflict?

Now my question, "what happens that forces someone to change?" implies both external and internal conflict. At this point in your planning, you may not know the internal conflict because that arises from character. In my mind, the plot and character work together to create the real conflict of a novel.

Later I'll talk about a pivot point—the midpoint—and how it can reveal the central conflict and/or theme. In very simple terms, a novel is a story of an event interrupting a person's life, and that person learns and evolves, and eventually changes. This is one way of looking at the central conflict.

It's okay to have a simple yet big external conflict at the center of your novel, such as a young father trying to save his toddler daughter from an obsessed ex-girlfriend. You can then layer a romance with another (sane) woman on top of that, give the daughter a serious health problem, and give the ex-girlfriend a very good reason to want to kidnap the little girl. That's a simple conflict that could happen in real life, and it opens up a world of hurt and problems for the characters. Throw in some personal issues (which should be related to the conflict) for them to grow through and overcome, and you have a strong premise.

Ideas with inherent conflict are easier to write. The more conflict, the more material you have to work with. Imagine a tattooed, bad boy biker who looks guilty of murder. Now add a justice-seeking female detective who is tired of fighting for every inch in a male dominated world. Maybe these two even crossed paths a few years ago in a bad experience that makes the Detective suspicious of him now, on top of the damning evidence. That gives you a heap of conflict to work with. Next you'll have to throw them together (while she's investigating) and have something surprising happen so she'll see there's more to him than the stereotype.

Your idea might be a genre story: a mystery with a cool setting, a romance with a crazy twist, or general fiction with a deep theme. Just remember, you'll have an easier time writing if you can clearly define your central conflict. Look at why your genre story needs to happen, and why your main character is the right person for the job. In a mystery, give the detective or cop a personal reason to solve the mystery. In romance, why are the two people uniquely suited for each other?

Conflict Exercises

#1. Think about your main conflict. By itself, does it have strong emotional appeal? Does it kick you in the gut or make you super curious? If it were a headline, would you read the article?

If not, can you make the conflict more meaningful through your character by giving them a personal stake? You might develop this more as you work on your idea and go through this guide.

#2. Does your main conflict suggest other conflict? Maybe the roles of your two main characters put them at odds.

#3. Brainstorm to develop your novel: describe your main conflict and free write or list consequences, results, complications. Anything goes. Multiple realities are allowed! Branch out to see all the direction your story could take. Follow ideas and see if they lead you to something strange, surprising, refreshing or satisfying. You might get some minor conflicts, new characters or subplots out of this, or maybe even big ideas for the main plot.

Step 3: Add Your Characters

If you can describe your characters and plot in one sentence, you've got a winner. At least, you've got a high concept that will guide you in writing and help you sell the story because others can see it too.

How do you do that? To start, think about the biggest trait for your two main characters and put that with their role or profession:

Aging professor (a bit cliché but a good example)
Innocent teacher
Naïve detective (a nice contrast)
Ambitious tattoo artist
Bitter ballet dancer
Hopeful prison warden
Angry birthing center nurse

Romance is full of types that readers love, and they don't seem to get tired of them:
Billionaire bad boy
Secret daddy cowboy
Wounded hero
Alpha male business owner

Having a super quick description of your character is helpful to keep in mind while writing your book. (Remember it's a starting point to build upon.) The best descriptions are less obvious ones. We've all seen the bitter, skeptical detective, right? Or the young, naïve woman who doesn't really have a life until a bad boy comes along. Go against the usual to make a surprising character.

Tip: Some writers like to find a picture of their character, either from a magazine or online, to help them write. That way you can confirm eye color or another feature with just a glance. It can also inspire you while writing to see your character. I like to find pictures that capture some emotion, like a pensive expression or big smile. Of course, you might not get a cover that exactly matches later on, but readers all have their own unique mental picture of a character anyway.

Once you have the short description for your two characters, put that with what they must face together.

An ambitious tattoo artist is a bone marrow match for the lazy landlord down the road. (Okay, that's a little weak but it gives you an idea of how to structure these.)

A naïve detective falls in love with a funny serial killer. (This loosely fits a movie called *Taking Lives* starring Angelina Jolie and Ethan Hawke, although she was CIA.)

Here's an example using my novel *All in my Head* again: Outgoing snowboarder Marcus Fields wakes up as a voice inside shy Avery's head where they can't hide their thoughts from each other.

If I want to expand it a little bit, I can add, "and they're forced to figure out if he has a body or if she's crazy, all while trying not to fall in love."

This tag line is very useful for promoting once you get to that stage.

Try expanding your description to include age and other helpful information. Let's create a short romance description:

27 year old Forest, an ambitious tattoo artist, is forced to mentor a bitter 24 year old ballet dancer Lily in order to stay out of jail.

I like this because Forest is ambitious but he needs to fulfill a court order to stay out of jail. So what did he do? And why is Lily bitter, when she's the younger one? And what did she do that requires her to work with a mentor?

Play Around with Character

Is your main character really the best fit for your plot? Once you plan more or even start writing, you can develop your character, but first I challenge you play around with the big elements of your character—look at the items that will be harder to change later on. I know it sounds like more work, but it can be fun to switch out your character. Imagine your story idea if you:

* Change the sex of your main character(s)

* Switch the role of the male and female in a romance: switch their jobs, who's the bad and good guy, rich and poor, etc.

* Change their family circumstance: two loving parents or an orphan, a great single parent or two really messed up

parents, two sets of parents, lots of siblings or none, nontraditional family structure... and the list goes on and on

* Change their career, money situation, social status, responsibilities...

* Look at their big personality traits and consider how the story would change if you mess around with those.

You may find a workable idea that strengthens your story, or thinking about some of these items might inspire you to add something smaller.

Another way to look at this is: Does the given trait do anything for the story? And if not, can you either make it do something to influence the story or change that trait/item so that it's more meaningful? Imagine if you can change the main character's career to it has a more symbolic meaning to the conflict they face.

Character Exercises

#1. Take your favorite books and movies and try to describe the main characters in a simple description. How would you describe Walter White from Breaking Bad? Or Harry Potter? One of my favorite TV characters is Jessica Jones. (And no, I'm not giving you the answers! There might be several answers to these. Just try to look at characters and see what their driving characteristic is. Some characters will have a few.)

#2. Try your plot with different characters to see how the story changes.

Can you switch in different occupations or roles to ensure you found the one that works best in your plot?

Is your character an overused cliché, like the bitter cop or naïve nun? If so, how can you switch it and surprise readers?

A side note: I clarified cliché with "overused" above because I think a cliché can be helpful in some circumstances such as a comedy, a starting point for a character who grows during the story, or a very minor character. Once in a while, I think readers enjoy recognizing a character as a common type they run into in real life.

Define Your Characters

We just worked on a quick description for your main characters. Now it's time to flesh that out. At this point, you might also change your characters and adjust your main plot.

Character makes story; the plot is just events. We read novels to see what happens to the hero, how they react and change, what they do about it, and what they learn. The biggest bestsellers are about strong characters, usually with inner conflict and tension that they live with until the plot forces them to face it.

A tip: plan your plot and character together, as two pieces of the same puzzle. If you give your character a trait, make it something useful to the plot. I've seen many writers create a character without the plot in mind, and then they weave little tidbits about the character into the story. Sure, these traits might be interesting, but they should either affect the plot or be a result of the plot.

It can be fun to create Character Dossiers or Sheets to keep all the important information together. I've seen many of these online for free, and the better ones include physical description but go beyond that. The aspects that make fictional characters memorable and unique are their conflicts, beliefs, histories, and inner battles. Your list might include:

* Name
* Age
* Occupation or role
* Social status or class

* Where they're from and where they live
* Biggest issue in life
* Biggest Hurt
* Biggest Fear
* how does their biggest fear play into goal and big threat?
* Goal in story
* Purpose in story

I often develop and change this while writing my first draft. Something will happen in the story, and I'll see an opportunity to incorporate a new fear or belief for one of the characters.

Writing helps me get to know my characters better. You might work that way, or you might write complex character descriptions before you begin. It's best to have something written down for reference. I'm discovering now that these lists are especially helpful when I'm working on a sequel and the first book isn't super fresh in my mind—this is very true with secondary characters.

Quick tip – check your character names to ensure they're not too similar, like Don, Dante and Devin or Shelly and Ricky and Cary. Our minds autocorrect more than we realize, and we can end up switching names on accident as we read if they look or sound alike.

You can flesh out your character sheet even more by looking at:
* Conflicting desires or beliefs (explained in questions at end of section)
* A wrong belief (include an explanation in the novel)
* A lie the character believed

* How they feel about each character
* A secret they share with one other character; even if it's small, this adds to the story

Plotting/ Character Tip: Look at your main conflict and work backward with your characters. Can you add a trait, belief, or past issue that will make the conflict even harder on your hero? For example, if the final climax is a battle in the night, can you make your hero afraid of the dark? Make it a good reason, like something really bad happened in the dark when they were young. Or if your hero has to swim to save someone in the end, can you make them afraid of water? Or if your hero has to become a public figure or make a speech, or do anything very public in the end, can you make them deathly afraid of that? These are fairly simple examples that hopefully will give you an idea of how to add complexity to your storyline.

An excerpt from 101 Questions to Improve Your Novel

*There are 19 questions for character development in *101 Questions*. Here are three of them that cover important topics. These can be used to check a finished manuscript or to help you plan.

Do your characters have good and bad qualities?

People are complex beings. We need to take care of ourselves and survive, but we also have a driving need to take care of others, especially our family and friends. All people have good and bad qualities, and those can change around different people or in different situations. Many famous characters are full of bigger than life qualities that might be quite annoying in real life. Can you list good and bad qualities for your characters? More importantly, can you show their good and bad qualities in the story?

Do your main characters have conflicting beliefs or wants?

Sometimes we believe a certain way until life comes in and complicates things. Try this on: a woman is 100% prolife and against abortion…and then her twelve year old daughter gets pregnant. How on earth can she reconcile her beliefs with helping her daughter? What should she do? That's a scary situation to even think about.

In fiction, you don't have to make a stand for either side of your character's beliefs. You might. Or you might just want to have a complicated situation for your character, and a chance to show how messy life is. "Conflicting beliefs" can be smaller issues too. Let's say your hero believes in always telling the truth. That's an easy one to test. Or maybe your hero feels bad about pursuing his goal because it means letting others help him, or taking from others, or leaving people behind that he cares about.

As authors, we get focused on our hero's motivation and goals: there is one big prize that will save the day. It's nice that fictional characters can focus on something bigger than paying the bills and cleaning the house, right? But what if that goal is complicated? If your hero wins, someone else might lose that same thing. Or, winning might mean crossing some personal lines or breaking a promise.

What does your hero want? Can you add something to your story that makes achieving that goal both a win and a loss? For example, what if your secondary character also wanted that prize for herself? Or, let's say your hero wants to win a boating race...but then his father can't win.

With a finished draft, you probably don't want to rewrite the story, but you can add in some doubt or other thoughts to complicate the issue. However, if rewriting your story would take it from so-so to amazing by adding in a big element, go for it!

Do characters change in a big way by the end?

Does your hero know something new or understand life in a different way? Can your hero do something they could have never faced or tried before the story opened? That is the heart of story: how the hero changes. Like life, this change can be small or subtle but still profound. The "big" usually means an inner change.

- If you feel your hero doesn't change, ask yourself:

- Does the hero finally accept that he (she) can be happy? (You can add this in with a few thoughtful lines toward the end.)

- Does your hero realize it's okay? Life is good?

- Can your hero come to grips with what they gave up?

You can also look at your conflict—did your hero fight hard enough and give up enough to reach the goal? Maybe your hero lacks change because you need to up the stakes.

Strong characters create conflict and make the story. If you pick one thing to focus on, choose the people populating your books. That will help the other pieces fall into place.

Step 4: Define Your Setting

Setting is more than just the time and place; it's the mood, season, people, traditions, holidays, languages and local history. Let's pretend for a minute that you're vacationing on the northern part of the Oregon coast. There's probably a seafood or berry or taffy or kite festival of some kind going on, or maybe several in different coastal towns. You stop in a small town and end up a few streets back, away from the tourists shops. A tall, bearded, flannel-wearing man is walking down the street. He's also wearing a black cap and thick, black glasses. You just came from Portland, so you assume this is another hipster. But in fact, it's a mill worker who's dressed like that all his life.

In this Oregon small town setting, you'd also encounter lots of people in camouflage, both women and men, who often drive big trucks. It might appear they're leaving on a hunting trip, but in fact they tend to dress like that a lot. It's just what's in their closet. Plus, hunting coats tend to be water proof so they're nice in the rainy weather here. That's one segment of the population. There's also hip, city people and ambitious business people and earthy hippies.

One thing you'll learn about Oregon is we like to recycle and think about the environment. Reduce, reuse, recycle. Sometimes I'll be at a public place and have an empty plastic container, but there's no recycling bin in sight. It's very, very hard to throw that into a garbage can. I'll pack that damn bottle around until I can recycle it. And it's funny, because this is normal to me, but I've met out-of-staters who thought the people were are "freaky" about recycling.

99.9% of the people here love to hike, camp, fish, and float the river. (I didn't actually research the exact number, but I think I'm pretty close. You can confirm this by reading dating profiles here!) Many of us own four wheelers and haul them over to the coast on a regular basis to run the sand dunes.

I'm painting one picture of life in Oregon, based on my experience living by Roseburg and Eugene in the middle of the state, in what is called either the "west" side or "wet" side because both apply. (Eastern Oregon is much dryer.) You'll get another picture if you visit Portland—maybe you've watched Portlandia?

So can all of that go into a novel? Maybe. Maybe not. Most of it would be background details, and the best way to show it is through the local characters. But if you get to know your setting, you can paint a unique world that will work to pull your readers into your story even more.

A common question for writers is, should they use a real setting or create a fictional one? Some romance writers create a fictional town and set a series there. It's a great idea, and Susan Mallery did this with great success. Other writers use a real setting that almost becomes a character in the book. You can probably think of a few novels that just wouldn't work in any other location. Have you ever read a book and wanted to visit that place? Or maybe you read the book because it was set in one of your favorite vacation spots.

For me, it's a given that I set my novels in my home state of Oregon. Of course, that's just the beginning. Oregon has so many different settings: on the coast, in the mountains, the bigger cities like Portland, Eugene, and Medford, or a small town. I've used both real and fictional settings. For real settings, I normally come out and name it, but once I used a real small town and named it something else in the novel. (It was fun when readers emailed to guess at which town!)

I don't take any kind of right or wrong stand on real verses fictional settings. There are pros and cons for both. It also depends on your genre. If you're writing fantasy or sci-fi, part of your job is creating a fantastical world. If you're writing mystery, some readers love the real setting and all its rich details about a city or place.

The one setting I don't like is the vague setting. It might be any city or any small town, and there's nothing to set it apart. That means your characters won't have any feelings about it, either, and you miss a layer in your novel. What if your hero has to return home to a town he hates, and his view of the town is slanted by that? Now picture a different character in a city she loves, and it's a real city that some readers might identify with and have feelings about too.

Sometimes a novel's setting is barely noticeable. It's in the background and doesn't change the story much. This works for a fast paced plot, but you can add so many interesting facts about setting in any story. Of course, you probably don't want to turn your novel into a lesson on a location, but you can add color and interest with local facts, filtered through the character's thoughts and experiences.

Before I talked about if an element in your novel actually changes the story. You can think about setting in the same way. If you change your setting, does it change the story?

Using Setting to Shape Story

If I hand you a novel and say it's set in the South, you probably get a good mental picture of the location, people, and way of life. What about the historical South? What about the Wild West or future civilization on Mars?

On a smaller scale, you can set your novel on a journey or even a road trip like *The Long Way Home* by Karen McQuestion. Do you remember Agatha Christie's mystery Murder on the Orient Express? What a great idea to use a train to force your characters to stick together. The same idea appears in *Water for Elephants* by Sara Gruen, set on a traveling circus for most of the story. The story also uses a retirement home, which could be another interesting setting. (Actually, *The Notebook* by Nicholas Sparks uses a retirement home in a flashback story the same way *Water for Elephants* does.)

My novel *Point Hope* is set in Coos Bay, Oregon, but it's actually mostly set inside the family's home. The story needed a lot of interpersonal drama for that to work.

I set *A Cowboy for Christmas* on a fictional horse ranch by the Oregon coast, so the ranch life shaped their activities. It's one of my earlier novels but it's a good example of using setting in a surprising way. Most people think of

Texas when they picture cowboys, so this mixed things up a bit.

I'm throwing out different ways to use setting so you can look at your story and consider if you can make your setting stronger. If you set it in a place you love, that will show in your writing. Or you might want to change your setting to somewhere rougher or grittier so it's harder on your character.

Setting Exercises

#1. If you haven't selected a specific location, brainstorm all the interesting places for your story to take place. Picture your story in different places to see if the new location would be more interesting.

Or, if you're writing fantasy or sci-fi, write out the rules and things that define your world.

#2. If you change the setting, does it change the story? If not, consider making your setting more unique or adding more "flavor" from your real setting.

#3. How can your given setting create more conflicts for your characters?

#4. Write a description of your setting, including the location, season, weather, time period, terrain of the land or feel of the city, the people, and anything that might add color to the story.

Step 5: Outline your Big Plot Points

Before we plot or map out your novel, let's take a look at the big plot points.

Many people break screenplays down into 14 or even just 7 points. You can watch movies to study story structure. And luckily for us, novels can be longer and more complex than a movie so you have room to develop your characters more, and time for subplots. Still, movies are an easy way to study plot points.

I studied the big bestselling novels of the last 15 years and came up with 7 main plot points for novels in my book, *Blockbuster Books, Broken Down.* These plot points work especially well for the young adult structure—like the books that went big and became movies. Following is a graph from Blockbuster Books showing the 7 points:

1. Opening threat or moment when "normal" is shattered

2. New Identity

3. New group (#s 2 and 3 are interchangeable)

4. The group fighting each other and coming together (or couple)

5. Big, black moment when all seems lost

6. Big showdown – the big action scene

7. Resolution

My Novel Structure

Traditionally, Act II goes to the climax and Act III is the resolution. I have Act II going to the midpoint, and then a whole other act between that and the big showdown. I redesigned my thinking this way because there is so much that happens in the middle of a novel between the Door of No Return and the Big Showdown, and many stories end up with a sagging middle.

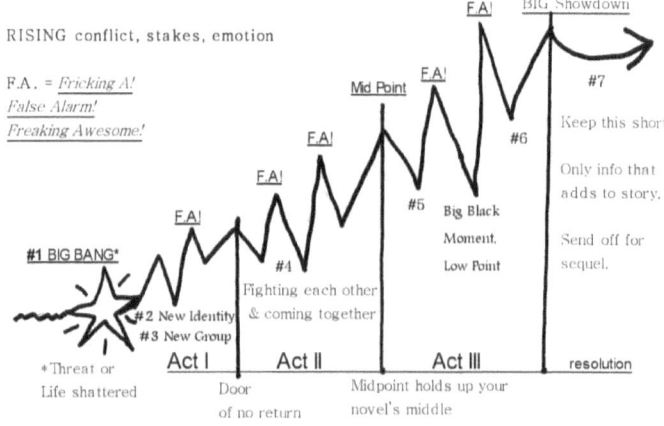

(A bigger view follows)

You'll have a few chapters for the beginning (Act I), the bulk of your chapters in Acts II and III, and a few chapters or even just one for the resolution. Longer novels of course have more chapters in every section, although the resolution should still be fairly quick.

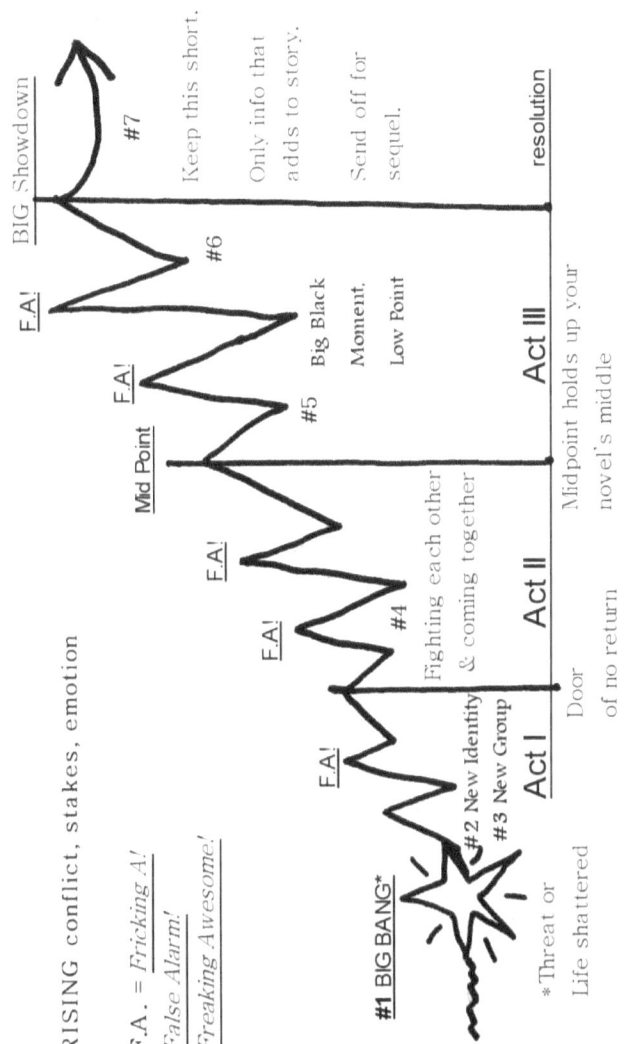

RISING conflict, stakes, emotion

F.A. = *Fricking A!*
False Alarm!
Freaking Awesome!

#1 BIG BANG*

*Threat or
Life shattered

#2 New Identity
#3 New Group

Act I

Door
of no return

Fighting each other
& coming together

Act II

Midpoint holds up your
novel's middle

Mid Point

#4

#5

F.A!

F.A!

F.A!

F.A!

F.A!

Big Black
Moment.
Low Point

#6

BIG Showdown

#7

Keep this short.

Only info that
adds to story.

Send off for
sequel.

resolution

Act III

The points rise higher and higher to show the growing tension throughout the novel, and the Three Acts are supporting posts. This avoids the awful "sagging middle."

I also added F.A. points to my novel structure, which can be good or bad points. (High and low points.) They stand for:

Fricking A! – Something really bad

False Alarm! – It looked bad, but turned out ok. Sometimes this is a trick or decoy too.

And Freaking Awesome! – These are the high points in the novel.

You may have many more F.A. points, and you may even have more than three acts. Bigger stories sometimes have long sections in a new location or with new characters, or big events that change everything.

Expanding the 7 Plot Points

Now you've seen the main points, so let's expand them to give you an even better idea of what to include in your novel. This is a good starting place and then we'll move into outlining and planning your novel.

Opening line – don't worry about this one yet. I actually like to jump into writing the story and then work on the first line later on in the process when I really know the character's voice and novel's tone.

Opening scene – this shows the normal world, but should have hints that things are not right. Or you can start in the middle of something happening already. That "something" doesn't have to be the big inciting event but it should relate to the story, such as showing your character in action at their job, interacting with other characters, or discovering something that sets things into motion.

Inciting event - Opening threat or moment when the sense of normal is shattered.

Scenes showing the effects of the inciting event – scenes where you reveal more information and complications

Interacting scenes, new Identity for your hero or both main characters – in YA, this is often an obvious new identity, like joining a group or learning about your destiny. In other genres, it's more subtle, but the character is changed somehow. They have a new case to solve, new information that makes the world seem different, a new job role, moving to a new location, or suddenly having someone to take care of, to list a few examples.

New group (#s 2 and 3 are interchangeable) – this is the new world that your character finds themselves in. Most novels have the hero go to a new place, or their current place is changed. This point is mixed into the developing scenes.

*Coming up on the end of Act I – you've introduced the characters and some conflicts, and began painting the main conflict of the novel. All this information is leading up to reveal something the hero/heroes must do or face.

Door of No Return – hero agrees to something, leaves on a journey, makes a decision, or does something that moves the story in a new direction. In romance, it's something that will put the characters together.

Act II - The group or couple fights each other and comes together

(In my novel version, this section leads to the midpoint.)

This is the fun section in a romance where the couple flirts, sasses, gets to know each other, and slowly realizes they have feelings for the other. Of course, they're fighting it and each other.

Low and High points, fun scenes

Complications – you can build on these and make them worse as the novel progresses

The characters start to see the value in each other and start to fear what they can lose.

Midpoint – decision time, commitment, acceptance, new direction

Taking action based on that decision – Readers will notice a change in your hero. It gives a feeling of momentum.

But obstacles galore try to stop them in their new mission.

Relationships get more complicated.

Everything gets more complicated.

Big, black moment when all seems lost.

A rally – yes, they will still fight (for the cause, for each other, for the goal)

Getting ready, preparing, finding allies, or finding new information

The Big showdown, climax, the big action scene, where they declare their love

Resolution

In general, novels all follow the same basic structure, but there's often so much on top of the structure that you don't really notice it. You just enjoy the story. So don't feel like following a structure will make your novel boring or predictable. The structure is what makes it a story.

Romance Novel Structure

This is a clean and easy structure for a contemporary romance novel like my titles that I've mentioned. They typically run around 50,000, but possibly 65,000 for romantic suspense or even up to 75,000 for the more complicated ones.

Act 1... (around 5,000 words)

Opening, normal world, might be set up for meeting

First meeting – sparks fly! They either are competing, or have old wounds between them—even though there is chemistry or feelings, they're not happy to see the other.

No! They fight against having to see each other, work together, be around each other, etc. They try to get out of it.

But, alas, they'll have to... (Door of no return, or simply door, or **threshold into Act II**.)

Act II... (around 20,000 words in this section)

Fun, flirting, sassing, arguing, getting to know each other, first kisses, fighting attraction but starting to see good points in the other.

(leads to...)

Point of no return (the midpoint, around 25,000 words into the book) – one or both makes some kind of commitment or deeper commit. They will go after the other, or make things right, or realize they love the other.

Act III... (around 20,000 words in this section. This is the 2nd half of Act II traditionally)

Complications, higher stakes, they start to really fall for each other

Now that they've made a bit of a commitment, they can get hurt easier. A lie? A betrayal? Something in the other's past? Or some new problem they're trying to hide? Leads to...

Dark Moment – (might be around 40,000 or 45,000 words into the novel) They give up on each other. It might be a big, ugly loud fight or a quiet disappearance. It seems lost.

One or both **rallies**, realizing how stupid they were, or they figure out a way to make it work, or they grow, but something changes.

They fight for the other (or both do)

Climax – it works, they win the other back!

Resolution – show the happily ever after

Step 6: Plan Act I to the Door of No Return

You have a good idea of novel structure now, and we've gone through some questions to guide you in creating your outline. Our first section begins with your opening and moves through Act I to the door of no return.

Outlining

If you haven't already, it's a good time to start laying out your novel. You don't have to write your outline from beginning to end, just as you don't have to write your novel that way. With a working outline, you can start with the big points and then connect them with smaller points. Of course, it might be easiest for you to work through your outline in order. Do whatever is most logical to you— you're already working to plan a novel so you don't want to struggle with the method on top of that.

Below is a simple outline showing the first chapter. I've kept the description short here, but it gives you an idea of structure and things to include. I also explain the purpose so you can see what I'm doing. When you outline and make notes on a scene's purpose, think about what it does for the story right then.

Example Outline

Contemporary Romance—the story's purpose is to bring two people together that are made for each other, but they fight it at first.

Act I – overview – Annie's house burns down and she meets her old flame, Mike. She needs to tell him something. He's an EMT and also builds houses, and he makes her an offer she really needs. She just doesn't want to accept his help.

Chapter 1 – overview - She just lost her father, her house burns down, one child is sick, and she feels like her life is falling apart.

Scene 1 – Annie leaves her father's funeral with her two young children. Her best friend Jenna helps with the kids, but one is a chronic illness that is acting up. Annie goes to bed wondering what else could go wrong.

Purpose – show her life as a single mom is a struggle but she's trying to make it own her own. (Her character motivation; she's the pillar for everyone else.) Intro Annie, kids, Jenna and Annie's life and home.

Scene 2 – She wakes to smoke and finds house on fire, gets kids, calls 911, then firefighters battle the flames but most of the house is lost.

Purpose – some things are out of her control, like losing her dad and her house burning down. Makes her vulnerable so Mike will be able to step in and help. Also tests her. Plus she'll need a place to stay. Handling the emergencies afterward gives the story structure.

Scene 3- She's sitting outside in ambulance, one kid on a ventilator, when she recognizes one of the EMTs as her ex-boyfriend Mike from 5 years ago. Little does he know this is actually his son that is helping...

Purpose – more complication for her child's illness, and the other child feels helpless and scared, intro the love interest and show how he helps people.

Chapter 2 - ....

You might have noticed there is a lot happening externally in this story. That makes it easier to write, and then the inner life of the character will really bring it to life. I could have started the story at the funeral and had a chapter of Annie's thoughts and reflections, but that can kill your beginning. It's better to have a beginning that moves and then sprinkle in the thoughts, feelings and backstory.

The job of your opening is to hook the reader and pull them in—make them curious! Don't explain your character in great detail or get bogged down setting up the story or world. Pretend that your story is already happening, and you're simply dropping the reader into it. They'll start running and following along, especially if you don't stop and explain everything.

What about Prologues?

This is one of those dividing issues: some preach against prologues like they'll sink your novel no matter what. And then some really successful authors use them. So is there an answer?

Well, we're just planning at this stage, so if you have an idea for a prologue, it won't hurt to write it down. It might turn into a first chapter, or it might be something you write and then cut, realizing it helped you get into the story and characters, but it's not needed.

If there isn't any reason to set it apart, consider if your prologue makes a strong first chapter. The point of a prologue is usually to show something earlier in time, but be careful of throwing down a bunch of backstory. It's more interesting to have that threaded through the actual novel.

How do you tell if your prologue works? You really don't need any prologue that isn't related to the story, so gimmicks are out. You also probably don't need it if it's dumping information. Even if it's critical backstory to the novel, you can work it in throughout the story as interesting tidbits. The exception might be if it's really interesting and engaging. I have one novel with a prologue called *Embers of Hope*. The prologue is a short scene showing a fire in an apartment building a few years before the story's opening. It's when the hero and heroine briefly meet, but it's just a chance encounter and they part ways. I went with a prologue because it opened the novel with a bang, included action, brought the characters together even though they didn't know it, and created an element of fate later on in the novel. It also brought the firefighter aspect out to front and center.

You might be able to remember a few prologues that really worked for you, and maybe some that didn't. Whenever you run into a "WRITING RULE" like this, consider readers. That's always your answer. Readers don't care about snobby rules from an editor. They love good stories. So ask yourself, will your prologue pull readers in and make them want more? Then it's a good thing.

That Opening Line

Again, we're just planning, so take a deep breath and relax. This is something to think about in the writing stage anyway, but I wanted to talk about the opening line along with beginnings.

When you do move on to writing, just start writing. Start with the first action or line of dialogue and keep going. Later on, you can come back when you're more familiar with your story and characters and write something that feels right.

My advice? Don't get too fancy with your first line. Don't write one of those "writer" sentences that will impress people. Instead think about what the character would think or say. I mean, come on, somebody actually started their novel with, "Call me Ishmael," and look how popular that book was. It's not about being fancy; it's about voice.

For fun, I just went to Amazon (literally, right now) and read the opening lines of the top selling books in Kindle. They're all pretty short, even five or six words. They don't dazzle me with the writing aspect, but I noticed they all jump right into the story. That's what you want. Because, truthfully, you don't ever want your writing to get in the way of the story or reader experience. If they want to have pretty poetry lines, they can read poetry. That's not to say you don't want to write well. Just remember you're not writing a paper for your English teacher.

I'd like to quote some opening lines of bestselling books but I'm careful about copyright. (And you can go study first lines in your genre and bestselling books at length.) I will share some of my opening lines:

Trey held an aged picture in one hand, rubbing a thumb over it. --*Point Hope*

"Maybe this is the one," Molly whispered, hoping against the odds that people in this town would know her. --*More Than Memories*

If her name meant anything to the tall cowboy who leaned against the porch rail, he didn't react. --*A Cowboy for Christmas*

Pretty simple and straightforward, right? These books have all done pretty well; they've been in the top 100 in Kindle and sold around 30,000 copies each.

I believe Stephen King gave the advice that your first line should invite the reader in. That's such a beautiful idea—your first line hints at a bigger story. I want my first line to intrigue and pull the reader into the second line.

Beginnings

Beginnings are hard. It's easy to overthink them, rewrite them like crazy, over edit, and then end up with an awkward passage that doesn't serve the novel. In fact, it might run readers off from a good story. My advice? Write the opening that feels natural and move on. Later, when the novel is written, it'll be much easier to tell if the opening matches the story's tone and starts in the right place. When you start writing, don't overwork your beginning and get stuck there. The opening is very important, but you'll have lots of time to work on it.

Do try to start as late in the story as you can, when something is already underway. (Take a look at my sample outline again.) You might even find that later on you want to cut your opening because it's too long and boring.

*Start the story with something happening, and avoid having a character waking to an alarm clock, starting their day, or daydreaming. (Yes, it does work once in a while, and you probably just thought of a successful novel that breaks one of these, but be aware that they're overused and often boring.)

*When you start writing, don't explain everything in the beginning. Write a scene that shows the characters doing something, and fill in a tiny bit of explanation, but try to slip that in throughout the first third of the novel in a natural way.

*Either start with the inciting incident or use an opening scene that shows some kind of unease–hint that things aren't right. Maybe your hero can tell something is off or about to happen.

*Don't throw every character at the reader in the first chapter. They need a little time to get to know everyone.

The first few chapters of your novel introduces your character, the important secondary characters, sets up the story's initial conflicts and possibly the big conflict, and shows the world of the story. The opening pulls your hero into something so they'll have to make a decision.

So you have your opening scenes and an inciting incident that changes life for your hero. This might make it easy for you to explain things to the reader. If the hero is thrown into a new environment, they'll have to learn about it, and the reader will learn along with the character.

An example:

Mark Wilson shows up at a lab for an interview. His potential boss greets him and gives him a tour. Oddly enough, he runs into an old flame who works there. (And we see that he applied here knowing that so it's not a coincidence.)

He meets the other characters, and you weave in his qualifications through dialogue or someone glancing at a sheet. But there are a few clues for the readers that something odd is going on. Mark starts to pick up on it, and then there's an explosion. (Or other event that shatters the illusion that things are normal.)

A situation emerges. Because we know Mark's qualifications, we know he has some training that makes him a great candidate to help. He knows something isn't right about all this, but he also has a strong reason to stay involved—his old flame. That takes you to the Door of No Return.

Genre Beginnings

One fun and exciting way to begin a romance is when the two people meet. That's what the reader is there for: the chemistry, the attraction and the excitement. Give it to them right away.

I've seen successful romances that have set up scenes, and that can be fun too—we see an event or several events happening and know it will bring our heroine into contact with some dashing male or bigger than life hero like a Marine or firefighter or even a bad boy. Then we get the payoff scene where they meet.

In mystery, you can open with a crime in progress to set up the world and show the genre, or you open with your detective or officer getting a call or showing up at the crime scene. Of course, you could do even better and go beyond the obvious for a unique way to start a mystery. Sometimes you can use a scene that shows the hero's life and their voice. If you can nail voice, you can do anything and get away with it.

Women's fiction often begins with some painful event that the heroine will need to overcome, or they're already dealing with the aftermath.

You should read and study your genre to see what really works and what you could do differently.

And just a thought: you can read openings all day long on Amazon, and take notes on what makes you want to buy the book.

"The Beginning" Exercises

#1. Do you want to portray "normal" in your novel's opening? If you do, how can you make it engaging? Can you show your character in action or really show off their strong voice? (In my sample outline with Annie, her "normal" is a hard life, and the story opens as she leaves her father's funeral.)

#2. What inciting event will shatter the "normal" you've established? (This would be the house fire in Annie's story—it pulls Mike back into her life.) I like to start my novels with the inciting event. Just drop your reader into the story and explain only as much as you need to.

#3. Does your hero find a new identity in Act I? A new role? What changes for your hero? This might be subtle or an official role change: New name, new job, new case, new person to protect, new location, etc. And does this role come with a new group?

Complications

The rest of Act I is development, explaining the story world, adding characters, and adding complications that take us to the Door of No Return and the end of Act I. This section of your novel might be a fun part, or at least where we get to know the characters and the world.

This part can be tricky if you haven't set up some action. Let's look at some other ways of setting of conflict with built in complications for your first Act. In my novel *A Cowboy for Christmas*, Missy shows up at a ranch on the Oregon coast to claim her share, left to her by a brother she hardly knew. She didn't know ahead of time that it was a half share, and the other half is owned by a cowboy with a wounded heart. After their initial confrontation, and Brent's acceptance that Missy would be there for at least a while, he has to show her the ropes. The ranch is struggling so he can't buy her out, and he actually needs another person, so she ends up working the ranch with him. That gave the characters something to do while they fought it out.

In *More Than Memories*, Molly shows up in her old hometown looking for answers...and lacking her memory. Right away, the local detective offers help, and we have this mini mystery of why he's so willing. Her reappearance opens a four-year-old cold case, so there's a bigger mystery to solve too.

In *All in my Head*, Marcus is stuck in Avery's head while she has to go to college and interact with her friends and her crush. That gave structure to the story.

If you set something in motion in the beginning, it makes writing Act I much easier.

The Door of No Return

Now that everything is changed, does your hero learn enough to push them to a decision of some kind, aka the door of no return?

Before the Door of No Return, Act I gave your hero just enough information that they can come to this point. It's been hinted at and set up. Now they have a choice.

As an obvious and easy example, picture a story about a group of Vikings heading out to sea to conquer a foreign coast. The first act might happen as they leave and spend a week on the boat—there might be fights between characters and the reader gets to know everyone. Then the Viking ship lands on the foreign coast and before invading, they burn the boats. That's definitely a point of no return.

In most stories, you won't have such a blatant door of no return, but the story will change direction. Think of Harry Potter going off to Wizard School.

In romance, there is some kind of commitment, job, project, task, mission, or trip that will keep the hero and heroine together.

In other genres, there is something that your hero will do or agree to that starts them in a new direction. It can even be something happens that forces them to get involved.

Sometimes you can actually be very obvious about the Door of No Return and other sign posts in your novel. Readers look for these points without thinking about it.

Now you're ready to jump into Act II.

Step 7: Plan Act II to the Midpoint

When I say "Act II" many writers will think of the entire middle of the novel, clear up to the climax. Remember, I cut Act II short so in my version, it extends from the Door of no Return to the midpoint, or middle of your novel. The main reason I think this way is to give more importance to the midpoint and create a pivot point in the middle of the novel. You can even view this subtle, small moment in the middle of your novel as your central theme because it's when your hero or heroine realizes what they really want and what they're going to do about it. Making Act II shorter also makes it more manageable to plan and write.

You've set the story up and now the real action is underway. What happens now that we know there's a threat or a mission? The characters have something they need to do. This section is about preparing for it, working the case, working on something together, or maybe just struggling through the recent and drastic events.

Your characters are bound together and have some understanding of what they're facing. This is a fun section where characters fight, vie for position, size each other up, form alliances, and eventually pull together. (At least, your "team" will pull together. You'll might other teams facing them or a villain.) These are high and low points.

Your character and/or team might set off on a literal journey or begin preparing for some upcoming battle.

Your hero is facing an inner battle as well through this section, and it propels them toward accepting their fate, falling in love, seeing their flaw, or changing in some way so they can make a stronger commitment at the midpoint.

When you think on a big scale, it can get overwhelming. I tend to think on a scene level by this point. What happens now? And how does that change the story, so what will happen next? Each scene is a new step, and it helps to keep your midpoint and ending in mind. (I'll talk more about scene building in the Writing section.) A practical way to develop this section of your novel is take the points, events, and threads in the beginning and take them one step further. Complicate everything a little more. Reveal a little more. Make things more complicated between characters as their relationships develop.

Act II Exercise

Building Conflict – list all the issues and conflicts from Act I, and for each one make a list of ways to make each item worse, or bigger, or more complicated. Sometimes it's simply a matter of developing the conflict a little more. You can reveal new information, introduce a secret, an alliance, or bring in some backstory that explains why this particular conflict is so hard for your hero.

Now that you're getting into the middle of your novel, what complications can you throw in? What high moments? How can you reveal and develop your characters more? In this stage, you're pushing your hero toward a decision at the midpoint.

Low and High Points

My novel structure (and most novel diagrams) show a zigzagging line that represents low and high moments, or scenes. In practical terms, it means to write a low scene (trouble, betrayal, frustrations, complication) and then a high scene such as a victory, new information, the characters having fun or making love, or something good happening. Often, when something really good happens, we know something bad is going to follow, and then we get that pay off when it does. You know that part in a show or movie when your characters are all laughing together as they drive a tank down the road? Someone's about to die. We all know it. We're all braced for the mine to explode. It's obvious, but it works.

This works in romance too, when the hero and heroine connect and have a really good scene… We know a secret or betrayal is about to come out or an old flame will show up to ruin things. It seems cliché but readers like set up and pay offs—it makes us feel smart and also satisfied that the story structure works as we expect. Now if the payoff is there, but somehow surprising, it's even better.

Midpoint

The midpoint is where your main character changes and turns toward the goal of the novel.

Around the middle of your story, your hero should make a subtle change. In the first half, they might not be fully committed to the fight. They've been fighting it inwardly, but something shifts. You can even picture your character facing the beginning of the story up to this point, but now they turn to face the big conflict head on. To illustrate, in my novel *Point Hope*, I had Trey move from wavering and doubt about what to do, to deciding to fight for his marriage and family.

In romance, one of the characters can make a decision to pursue the other.

Do you have a midpoint in mind already? If you don't, it's often something you realize after writing most of the novel. This is a small moment, yet very important. But because it's small, you can work backwards later on and add it after you've built your character arc. Just keep it in mind for now.

Step 8: Act III: Plan the Middle to the End

Under the traditional three Act structure, you might find yourself lost in the middle, unsure about how to keep things exciting until the climax. That is why it's so helpful to picture a point at the middle of your novel, holding it up.

Now your hero has really committed to the mission. They found a personal reason to. In the beginning, it might have been a call to save the world or help someone, but now something very personal is at stake.

Taking Action

The great thing about your hero realizing something, making a decision, or making a commitment, is that now they need to take action. It's like a wave of energy rolling into the novel, and like a real wave will carry you into the beach, the midpoint commitment will drive your hero toward the climax. This gives your story more structure and helps you plan out the second part of your novel's middle.

Again, take all of your conflicts, story threads, sub plots and complications, and plan out how you can develop or worsen each of them.

Remember to still use high and low points. A fun way of doing this is to look at your scenes and determine the dominating emotion. Now throw in a scene that breaks that up. If your novel is very serious, can you have a lighter, even funny scene?

Look at your story arc - Do your conflicts increase after this? Are things getting worse? Life should be harder and harder from now on, but your character more determined. Things get worse and worse until we reach the Dark Moment.

A tip for planning scenes – each scene is another point that will lead to the end. Scenes are links. If you picture a chain, each link is connected to the one before and the one after. In a novel, a scene can satisfy questions from earlier, and bring up new questions for future scenes. If a scene feels too "wrapped up" and doesn't have any tension, give your point of view character doubt about what he/she is hearing, doubt about the other character's intentions, doubt about something on their mind, or some unease that will foreshadow something to come.

Dark Moment

Your character has been working toward an external goal but runs into all kinds of problems. This chips away at their resolve and worsens their internal conflict as well. You have to push them to their breaking point—it's the internal conflict that brings about the dark moment when they consider giving up.

Do you have a dark moment where all seems lost? How can you make it even worse? To create this, you can throw one crisis after another at your hero until they're broken. (But then they're not.) They might actually give up during the dark moment and then rise again.

After the dark moment, your characters have to rally. This is similar to the midpoint. It can even be an affirmation of the midpoint, when the characters digs down and remembers why they decided to go down this path. Of course, they've learned a lot about themselves and life by now, so they have even more reason to fight.

Climax

Do you see your climax? Do you know what the big conflict really is, and how it can be finally resolved? Brainstorm big events and try to create something that's not obvious.

Tip - While planning and writing your novel, keep track of all the conflicts that need resolved and different threads in the book. I sometimes make a separate document to list items like this, and then I can look through it as I finish writing the novel.

You might even want a separate file to outline your subplots. (Side stories, threads that only involve one main character, or told through a secondary character.)

Resolution

So you have your big climax… then what? It's time to wrap up. This is that little chocolate after dinner. It's when the characters get to look at each other and say, "We made it! Well, of course we made it!"

Check your list of conflicts and subplots. Did you wrap everything up? Do you need to explain anything? (You might do better by adding something in before this point, but not always.)

The main purpose of the resolution is to give readers that satisfying feeling of completion. It's even better if you can leave them staring at the book, wondering how to go back to real life.

We have that saying, *they rode off into the sunset* for a reason: it shows that they reached a happily ever after, and that they will continue on. Different genres have different expectations. If you're writing romance, you better have a HEA or be prepared to face reader wrath. I know this from personal experience! I originally ended *All in my Head* on a bit of cliffhanger. It wasn't enough of a HEA for my romance readers and they let me know. So I wrote an epilogue and started a sequel. They did forgive me, and quite a few updated their review on Amazon on Goodreads. (Aren't readers awesome?)

If you read romance or follow publishing at all, you might remember the outcry when the last book released in the Divergent series. I won't give anything away, but readers were angry. Like, surprisingly and violently angry! That's how passionate people are about novels and characters that they love.

When I write my endings, I'm all emotional over the story and how things have turned out for my characters. If I get that chest-swelling, even teary-eyed response, I feel good about sharing it with readers.

Your beta readers can also tell you if the ending fulfilled your story promise.

Ending Exercises

1. Can you make your ending surprising in some way?

2. Can you also fulfill genre expectations and maybe some things that feel cliché? That sounds strange, I know, but your ending should have a little feel of familiarity, meaning it *feels* like an ending.

3. Does the emotional tone fit the story and ending? Look at your genre, your other novels if you have any, and the story itself to see what kind of emotional tone you should use.

4. Can you remember any endings that left you feeling cheated? If so, why not go study why they didn't work.

5. Can you remember any endings that blew you away? Study those too of course!

6. Does your ending satisfy the story threads but also give a sense that the characters will go on with their lives?

The Last Line

This is just something to think about for now. Or, actually, you don't have to think about it yet. Plan and write the story, and then you'll get the rewarding, emotional, amazing experience of typing that last line. I think the last line comes easier than you'd expect. You know the characters and your main character's voice. You know the tone and feel of the story. You can imagine how the character would sign off. You might even have the main character speak the last line.

The last line is a little kiss goodbye – it should fit the story and send readers off with a feeling of wanting more of your books.

And luckily you have millions of novels available to you to study last lines.

Step 9: Writing

Here's the big payoff for all your planning! How do you actually go from thinking and planning to writing a novel? I already told you the secret that the planning and foundation really affects a novel's success. The secret to succeeding at *writing* one is to write it one scene at a time. If you write one great scene, and then another, and another, you'll soon have a novel. Let's say you only have an hour a day before or after work. You can write one scene a day, equaling around two chapters a week.

A few tips to start your writing time:
* Read the previous day's scene to get back into the story
* Read over your notes in your outline on the scene and its purpose
* Consider writing a quick overview of what you plan to write that day. (You might not need this if your outline is detailed enough.) This can be a quick note scribbled on your notepad or something on your computer. I consider it a to-do list that I can check off, and it helps to focus me. Sometimes this list includes story questions or some little detail that I want to work in as well as the scenes I want to write.

Scenes are critical in a novel, and while that seems obvious, I see a lot of confusion around what a scene is when I'm editing. Have you tried to write a novel before and struggled, and maybe didn't finish? If you can, go back and look at your outline. (If you didn't have planning of any type, that could be part of the problem right there!) In your outline, did you list scenes? And did you have notes that talked about the purpose of each scene? When you wrote it, did you think about what needed to happen in each scene and why?

A scene is a step. It not only adds a step to the story, it points to future steps. If you have a clear purpose for your scene, you'll stay on track. Without a purpose, it's easier to get sidetracked on description, backstory, conversation that doesn't move the story, or writing a section that doesn't serve the story. With a purpose, you can add in things and layer them, and still check to ensure you've accomplished the scene's purpose and move the story closer to the next big event.

Marking Scenes

It's very helpful if you can mark your scenes and important events or items so you can easily find them. That way, if you're working in one spot and have a question, you can find the spot with the answer.

I write in Word, and I mark each scene as a Heading 2, and then I open the Navigation Pane (under "View" up top) so Word will put an outline to the left of my document. I sometimes also insert a Table of Contents at the beginning so I can see my outline there. Many authors use Scrivener for this, but I like Word better. It's all about personal preference. You can also write an outline, make a copy file, and fill that out with your novel.

The one catch with my method is that I have to go through and remove the scene headers when the book is finally done. To do that, I make a new copy of the book so that I still have a file with the scene markers. (Sometimes I go back and use that to find something.)

My scene names are what the scene accomplishes, and this can come straight from your outline. These might include, "Marcus confronts father" or "Avery confides in Jazz." They're fairly simple and straightforward, but these tags let me know exactly what needs to happen in that scene. I include these inside of scenes as well to mark things like, "first mention of Nash" or something that I know I'll want to be able to find later.

Writing Scenes

How long should a scene be? Mine range from 1500 words up to 4,000 for the really long ones. It's not about word count, though. The more important thing, and what readers notice, is if the scene is complete. I like to have three scenes per chapter or one longer one, or one that's really significant.

If you picture a novel as a domino tower, each scene is a new domino. It takes the story another step. That means a scene:

*has a beginning, middle and end
*has a purpose

*adds something new to the story so that deleting the scene would change the story

A scene's opening doesn't have to ramble on, describing the setting in great detail. However, you should paint the scene with at least a few key details that reveal more than the physical appearance. Can you hint at the tone and emotional atmosphere with your word choice?

Clue readers into who is there early on. Don't you hate it when you're reading along and suddenly a character speaks or does something, and you didn't even know they were there? (It's different if a character does suddenly appear, surprising the other characters and the reader. Just don't do it on accident!)

Use actual dialogue as much as possible instead of summarizing. It's good to show thoughts too, especially when they contradict the dialogue. Action is good, and can work as a tag instead of "said" over and over. You can also use action to contradict what's being said. Maybe a character says something while folding their arms, blinking, looking out the window suddenly, looking down, or turning away.

Have some kind of conflict in each scene. Remember, each scene should change the novel, so you'll have an argument, new information, two people who don't agree on a very basic level, two people who don't like each other, or rising conflict between characters. The exception might be your high point scenes—and those imply conflict because readers instinctively know something will happen to shatter that, or you can hint and foreshadow.

If a scene is simply there for transition, consider cutting it. You don't have to show a car ride, a meal, or anything that is normal and routine. You can always skip ahead and start a new scene, and simply show where and when the story is. Or, if you want to keep the scene, add a second purpose to it.

Should you write every day?

I've heard of writers who say they write every single day, even weekends. Many have a regular weekday writing schedule. Some people write in the evenings because that's when they feel creative. I think it comes down to personality and life factors.

When I'm excited about a story, I want to write on it all the time. It helps to work on your novel often to keep it fresh in your mind. When I step away from a project, it gets stale and the characters don't feel as real.

However, the better question might be, *can* you write every day? Most people, especially when they start out, write when they can.

But you also have to take care of yourself and avoid burnout. I can't write seven days a week all year long. I get tired of sitting, my fingers actually get sore from typing too hard, and then there's eye strain. (I know there's ways to work around those with things like verbal dictation, a standing desk, etc., but I like to sit and type when I write.) I can get mental burn out too, and then I need a fun trip or a few days off to recharge.

My advice is to have a schedule and stick to it, but don't get down on yourself if you need to be flexible. Look at your weekly and monthly word count instead of basing how you feel on that day's writing.

Should you set a daily word count goal?

Most writers find this very useful. I tend to set a weekly goal because I'll write more on one day, less on some days, and possibly take a day off from that given project or off of writing all together. However you do it, a goal will help you stay on track with your novel.

Instead of a word count, you could also set a chapter or scene goal, or even a time goal. Say you have an hour every day to write. Take that time and do what you can, and don't get down on yourself if you write 500 words or just 100 on a hard day. If you're writing, you're making progress.

As an exercise, you could chart your daily word count and when you write. This can show you some surprising things, like when you're most productive.

Should you write in order?

There are countless ways to plan a novel and countless ways to write one. Don't let anyone tell you there is a right and wrong way because it's a creative process. Every author develops their own way of doing things.

It makes sense to start at the beginning and write to the end. That way, you can keep the story in your head in the correct order, right? This method is great if it works for you. You can look at your outline and chapter/scene notes, scribble down what you'll write that day, and go for it.

But what if you get stuck? Let's say you've written three chapters and suddenly lose your motivation, or the story feels confusing. That's actually a natural occurrence once you get into the novel a ways. You have a lot of story threads to juggle, after all. But if you really can't write a scene, skip it. That's why you have an outline: to keep the story straight and in order. Go to a scene you really want to write and let your passion shine through. Sometimes you can write the entire rest of the novel and then come back to the troubling scene or scenes, and figure out why you don't want to write it.

If you really struggle to write a scene, it might end up meaning that readers won't want to read it. There's something lacking there. It might be a boring scene that you think you need for a transition or to reveal some information. Maybe you don't need that transition. Just start a new chapter or a different scene. And if that boring scene has critical information, just work it into another scene. Check the scene's purpose to see if it really works, or if you need to clarify what that scene does.

If you have your story planned out, you can actually write the big scenes first to ground the book. I've written my endings when I had only half of the novel done. If you do this, just know you might need to edit these scenes later on to match the story. (But you'll be revising and editing anyway.)

Should you edit and revise during the first draft?

Most people agree it's best to stick to writing to get a first draft completed. You don't want to spin out and spend a year editing and reworking the first third of the novel.

That said, when you start writing every day and read over the previous day's work, you might edit a little. That won't slow you down much, and it gets you back into the story. You can also finish a scene and read through it to edit and add. That's different than endless editing without new writing.

Sometimes I'm writing and realize I need to add set up for my current scene, or I just get an idea of a little thing to add to another part. I have my outline open in the navigation view to the left, so I jump to that part and either write the new content or make a note. Or, I might just jot the idea down on a piece of paper next to my computer and keep writing.

Staying in the flow

If you're happily writing away and run into a problem or question, you can mark that spot with an XXX or other symbol that you can search for later on. I might highlight something to tell myself to double check it (like a character's eye color or name spelling for a minor character) or I might use Word's comment feature to write down ideas and reminders. Some of my comments might read, "Does this make sense with the fight in chapter two?" or "Does Avery actually know this at this point in the story?" I'll leave a comment for anything I need to check, or if I should add something to another part of the story. Doing this allows me to keep writing and making progress, and later I can spend some time going over these items.

Keeping up your momentum

One common writer's trap is to get bogged down in editing during the writing phase. This happens when you have part of your novel done but you start reading through it and rewriting instead of writing new material. It's fine to do some of this, but if it stops your progress, you might never finish. I've met writers who've spent years on the same book. Some writers work that way. Some really great writers work that way. But you probably want to finish your rough draft and then edit. I love that phase when I have a full novel to fine tune.

If you want to edit while writing, consider going over only the previous day's writing at the beginning of your writing day. That can serve to catch any issues and refresh the story in your head.

Celebrate your progress

Celebrate when you reach a new milestone: 10,000 words, 20,000 words, 40,000 words, a finished draft. It can be hard to work on a novel without knowing how it'll do later on. It's a gamble. You're putting your heart and soul into it, so acknowledge that hard work and dedication.

Remember, once you get your story down on paper, you have material to re-organize, edit and revise.

Step 10: Re-writing & Editing

So you have a finished manuscript. Hooray! Congrats. You should celebrate before moving forward with polishing your work. Savor that feeling a bit. And then get pumped up for the next stage.

This section provides a good overview of the polishing stage. Afterwards, if you want to go even deeper, consider reading my book *101 Questions to Improve Your Novel*. I've used a checklist for several years that listed everything I had learned about story. I added an explanation for each item and turned it into a book to share with others. Now I actually use a copy of the book instead of my checklist.

There's a funny rule I used to hear a lot, that we should stick the manuscript in a drawer for three months and forget about it, and then go back with fresh eyes. I have a feeling the rule came from an editor for some reason. So this *could* be good advice for some writers. It doesn't work for me because then I have to familiarize myself with the little plot details and timeline again, and it makes more work. I like to have my stories fresh and my characters alive in my mind. I also want to finish a project before moving on, and if I put a novel away, I'll start working on another. So it depends on how your brain works, your timeline, and your goals.

I also really love to get to the polishing stage, where I get to make the book even better. I tend to add layers, more description, little hints, and tie things together even more.

Do what works for you. If you need a break, take one. But don't think you have to take a three month break simply because someone made a rule.

There are a few ways to begin the revision process. You might do a read through yourself, checking the flow, development, and writing. Some writers like to print out their story so they can mark it up. Quite a few people have told me they catch things on paper that they don't see on the screen. Other writers like to have other people read through their novel and give feedback. For me, I want to read through on the computer where I can edit and add for the initial read through. I wait until I'm to the proofing stage to either print it out or read it in Adobe so I won't start editing again.

I go over chapters during the writing process. So when the novel is complete, I've gone through most or all of it many times. (I go back and forth, writing in different places and checking spots.) Once I feel like the novel is a complete story and fairly revised, I pull out my writing books and do a workshop at home, checking different things. I also use my book, *101 Questions to Improve Your Novel.*

So how much rewriting, rearranging and editing will you have to do? How do you evaluate your novel? You probably want feedback, but you might also want to do some checks yourself to ensure it's the best story you can provide to beta readers. So onto the next question...

There is more than one correct answer on when to share your work. A newer writer might want to share chapters from a work in progress, if the reader is someone who can offer valuable feedback. For example, if you're a member of Romance Writers of America and you can have a mentor read your chapters while your novel is in progress, you can feel pretty good about the feedback. I'd recommend doing that. You might also know an author with more experience than you who is willing to critique your novel. Just be careful that you don't get stuck in the editing trap, and be especially careful that you're not asking the wrong people for advice.

Readers might all suggest different things. Ask yourself, do they read in your genre? Do they have any writing experience? Are they being overly nice because they're super supportive? Or, on the other hand, are they being overly critical because that's how they always treat you?

Don't be too hard on readers if they're not trained to offer feedback. Sometimes, all they can tell you is that they liked it, didn't like it, or liked certain parts.

Normal readers, such as friends and family, can probably tell from your beginning if they want to read on. A hired professional can point out your strengths and weaknesses, missing plot points, character problems, and things with pacing. I've looked over a lot of manuscripts, and I'm often surprised by the story elements, characters or writing, and also by the different and unique writing issues. There are some common ones for sure, but writers are so different too. It can really be fun to help another writers develop their style and voice, and use their strengths.

On that thought, when you give your work to others for feedback, ask for their overall impression and also a specific list of things. This could include your concerns and questions related to any known strengths and weaknesses.

Consider asking beta readers to write their reaction at the end of each chapter or scene break—even if it's just a quick note or even a smiley/frown face to let you know if they liked that part.

A few more questions to ask beta readers:
* Would you read past the opening? The first chapter?
* What do you like about the story?
* Do you like the characters? Can you relate to them?
* Do character actions make sense?
*Did any part confuse you?
* Are there any parts you skimmed or wanted to skim?
* Does the pacing feel right, meaning does the story move and keep your interest?
* Do you see any writing strengths and weaknesses?
* Does the writing ever distract you from the story?

You may have noticed these are a little more general than what you'd pose to another writer or someone with critiquing experience.

If you're around writers much, you know they're always looking for critique groups or partners. These can be highly beneficial or a complete waste of time, or anything in between, completely depending on your group and how you interact and utilize it. I've found some groups will focus on the tiny details, so you'll take in a story and all the feedback is about a typo on page two. That's not really all that useful. Other times you get all kinds of feedback that's different. If you do get meaningful feedback, and from several members, it's time to take a look.

I love to hang out with other writers, so writing meetings and critique groups can be fun and useful. I just advise to think about who is giving you feedback, what they're focusing on, and their level of experience. Another factor to consider is the purpose of the group—I'm a working novelist, so I want to strengthen my novel and get it ready to publish. Some groups have writers who have been working on their novel for ten years, and they don't plan to look for a publisher or publish any time soon. There are different kinds of writers, and you want to find a group that's somewhat similar to you in speed, purpose, goals, and personalities.

You can guide a critique, too, by stating what you're worried about or asking questions.

If you find a group to join, it's usually a little bigger. If you start a group with people you already know, however, you might be able to have a small group of three to five people. In a smaller group, you can focus more on each person's work. This is especially true if you have a critique partner. You get to know the person's writing style and can really help them grow novel to novel. Many successful writers have a trusted "first reader" or a writing/critique partner that gives valuable feedback. They don't have to write in the same genre either. Sometimes it just takes trying out different relationships to find the right match.

Start with the big issues

When I critique and/or edit a novel, I have a list of things I look at in addition to pointing out the writer's strengths and weaknesses if I see any. This is my list, starting with the bigger items:

* Plot and character development
* Story order, structure, and development
* Dialogue – ensuring it sounds natural
* Passive voice, mixing of first and third or tense problems
* Description
* Overused words
* Summary (show don't tell)
* Pacing, slow movement, unneeded scenes
* Unrealistic details that throw readers out of the story
* Repeated information, conflicting information in different parts
* Point of view problems (skipping around, "head hopping," unclear point of view)
* Lengthy paragraphs or chapters

The big elements and issues are plot and character development, and then story order, structure, and development.

Reading *a lot* will give you a feel for novel structure and pacing.

You can work on your plot by crafting a strong outline. If you kept your outline updated to the finished novel, you can use it to check story order too. (It really comes in handy to use the headers in Word or scene labels in Scrivener, and then you can see your story structure at a glance.)

Next you can work on character development on a scene level. I take one character at a time and go through the novel to look at their point of view scenes. (Meaning they are the main character and telling the story.) I try to see how I can develop their thoughts, the inner conflict they feel in that scene, and how they feel about the other character.

Checking Smaller Elements

When I say "smaller" elements, I don't mean less important. I use the term smaller because these are easier to fix. They work on a writing level instead of structural level. Here's my list again, with an explanation for each item.

Dialogue should sound natural but not too natural. Fictional dialogue shouldn't sound like real speech, but mimic it. We don't speak in long paragraphs. Grab a book by one of your favorite authors and highlight the dialogue. Try this with several authors who have different styles.

Passive Voice – If you can add "by zombies" the end of a sentence, it's passive. You can search your file for words like *were* and *was*.

Mixing of 1ˢᵗ and 3ʳᵈ person – this can happen if you write a lot and your different projects have different point of views, or you're starting a new project in a new person. It should stand out while reading through or editing, and you can search for certain words to check it too. If your novel is in first person, you can search for she and he, her and him, to see if you slipped into third person.

Tense problems – this is another one I tend to do when switching projects. If you're focused on one novel, you might have less trouble with these! I think a tense problem is harder to catch than slipping between 1ˢᵗ and 3ʳᵈ person. Sometimes I'm writing in the past tense, but when my characters think, it's easy to slip into present. (I even do it on purpose a little... you can play around with some things are you gain more experience.) You can search "ed" to find past tense, but you'll get a lot of other results too.

An editor should see both of these when they edit.

Description – it's all about the right details. These days, readers don't want a page of description for each new scene, unless you're writing regency. Genre will dictate a lot about the description in your novel. Fantasy and science fiction might need more, while action novels need less. Most readers want enough detail so they can imagine the scene – what's the feel of the setting, the unique details that reveal something, and what does the character notice and feel? A few strong details can really paint the setting, especially if they're infused with emotion and possibly even action. Here's a quick example:

The conversation dropped dead as I entered the tiny, 70s themed kitchen. A fan blew in the window but the weak breeze didn't fix the stench of old garbage and coffee grounds floating in the hot, moist air. Allan stood leaning against the cluttered counter, and sent Devin a quick glare before looking at me. Devin had been rocked back, but he set the rickety wooden chair flat again and started picking at bread crumbs on the table. While I searched for words, a rat ran across the floor and the three of us watched it.

Description is a powerful tool if you use it to set the mood and reveal character emotions.

Overused words – Most writers have a word or two, or some phrases, that they overuse. I have a list for myself and I'll search through the entire book to mix it up.

Summary (show don't tell) – you can catch this one sometimes because there's large blocks of text. Other times, you read a section and realize you could actually show that conversation or scene, or simply cut it and jump into the next scene. You don't always need a transition. Another way to catch this is to ask yourself, is the scene or section painted for the reader, or does it read like someone is telling you something?

Pacing – Do you hit the main plot points in around the right spots? (Refer to the novel structure diagram for this.)

Slow movement – do you get lost in description, conversations that read like everyday interactions, or grind away at the same conflict without escalating it?

Unneeded scenes – these might be "pretty" scenes that don't add to the story, or transition scenes that don't matter, such as a car drive or getting to one place or another, or long thinking scenes where nothing new is revealed. Sometimes you can rewrite these and add in another conflict, reveal information, or introduce a new doubt. Other times, you just don't need them and can cut them.

Unrealistic details that throw readers out of the story. Have you ever been reading along and suddenly something jars you right out of the story? You can tell the author didn't do their research. I'm sure we're all guilty of this at one time or another in our writing, and sometimes the reader may be the mistaken one. Still, it's best to research. When writing, you can highlight or mark something that you don't know that well, and research after your writing session. A good editor will point out some of these and mark places where they think something might be off too.

Repeated information – this one isn't as common, but sometimes you'll pound something into the reader. Editors will mark it RUE, or resist the urge to explain. That's when you show, and then tell, and then maybe explain too to make sure the reader got it. You can trust readers to understand.

Conflicting information in different parts – Beta readers are good at catching this. Your character starts the day in a skirt and ends up in pants, or eye color changes, or some plot detail shows up differently.

Point of view problems (skipping around, "head hopping," unclear point of view) – We already discussed slipping between 1st to 3rd person. You can also accidentally include a thought from a non point-of-view character. I think this isn't as common as it was – authors used to use the omniscient point of view and share everyone's thoughts, but the close, first person has become much more popular.

Lengthy paragraphs or chapters – this is easy to check by shrinking the page and glancing through, or noticing long paragraphs when you're doing a read through.

Should you have a theme?

This is a tricky question because we're not always sure what a theme is. In my mind, it's simply a subtle message that your story conveys. It can reinforce something good about mankind, and it can be very simple. Do you think the Harry Potter series has a theme? We could come up with several, but a strong theme (to me) is the importance of friendships.

Most of my novels don't have a strong theme, although you could argue that the theme of romance is that love conquers all. I like to write stories that show love is worth fighting for. It's not a huge revelation but it confirms in readers something we want to believe. This is stronger in some of my novels, such as *Point Hope*. The idea of the story is that love and family are worth fighting for, even when you have every reason and right to give up on someone.

A better question about theme might be, do you already have a theme? It might be there, embedded in your story. In my opinion, if you have a theme that you can strengthen, great! But if you try force a theme, it can come off as preachy or stick out like something you decided to tack onto the story.

So how do you show theme in your novel? It can be something you think about while writing. You can give a character a few lines of internal thought about it. You can even have a character announce or declare theme to another character: "I'll do whatever it takes to keep you alive because I love you!"

In *Point Hope*, and I had the main character Trey give a speech near the end, basically telling the other characters and the reader the point of the novel. You've probably seen this in movies. It might be a speech near the end or the character thinking about what they learned. In a movie, it's the voice over at the end. Pretty easy, right? Just keep it subtle, which ironically makes it stronger.

When is your novel finished?

Now this is a complicated question. First, let's define "finished" as a fully developed novel that you've polished to the best of your ability. It means you're ready to have it edited and then proofread.

Your novel isn't done if you find yourself thinking, "It's good enough." Or, you're just exhausted and done working on it. If that's the case, you might need a break so you can come back fresh.

You can feel good about a novel if:
* You planned using plot points
* Worked on plot and character development
* Developed your characters on a scene level

* You feel the story is complete and the character(s) have a fully developed arc where they change
* You used writing resources such as books by experts to go through your novel (or hired professionals)
* Got feedback and revised (and considered the source of the feedback)

I think we can get caught up in the technical aspects and worry that someone will find something "wrong" with our novel. I understand that, but, at this stage, consider the story. When it's ready, you can work with an editor on the small things. When you've edited and polished your novel, remember to celebrate that step too! You've done a lot of hard work. It's an accomplishment to finish and polish a novel.

Wrapping Up

Down the road, you'll look back and realize you've learned a lot and could possibly make an early novel better. But it's a snapshot of your ability, too. I see elements in some of my novels that I could fix now, but I still really love those stories and characters. The writing journey is...well, a journey. You learn and grow. You might worry over the technical aspects of your novel, but the more important thing is, did you let your passion for the story shine through? Readers want good stories, and they'll come to your book hoping to love it. I wish you the best of luck in your writing journey!

Also by Kristen James

I've talked about my other nonfiction books in this guide, and I'm including their descriptions and Table of Contents in case you're interested in reading more.

Blockbuster Books, Broken Down

 The fun guide to plotting: Learn from mega bestselling novels to build your own breakout plot!

Why start from scratch and reinvent storytelling? Instead, use a 7 point plot outline developed from wildly successful novels.

"Blockbuster Books, Broken Down" is a workbook style guide that reveals the structure and elements in huge bestsellers of the last fifteen years, many of which became movies. By breaking down these books, we can see how successful authors are breaking out by satisfying readers' needs.

Part 1 deconstructs today's bestsellers and offers insights and keys to blockbusters and the Blockbuster Novel Map.

Part 2 guides you in creating a breakout idea and developing that into a solid plot with a novel map. Build from the ground up with 7 points to ensure your plot will connect with readers.

From plot twists to dialogue, authors have a long list to think about when revising and polishing a novel. These 101 questions and explanations will help you improve and check your novel's opening, plot and character development, conflict, pacing, dialogue, and of course the writing itself. After months or years of working on a story, it's difficult to check the quality on every fiction element. 101 Questions looks at overarching issues, small details, and writing technique. You may learn about new techniques and tips, see a method differently, or realize that you forgot a trick. This handy list of 101 questions explores many possible ways to improve specific areas, add layers and depth, strengthen conflict, find plot holes, and identify writing issues.

All About Story
All About Editing
The Beginning
Plot & Structure
Characters
Chapters & Pacing
Scenes
Dialogue
Setting and Description
The Ending
Strong Writing
Final Checks
Share Your Book!

Authorpreneur

Authorpreneur: a noun. A professional author/entrepreneur who strives to improve in all areas of the publishing business: writing, publishing and marketing.

What does it really take to make it as an author? What are realistic production and promotion costs? Do many people make money publishing ebooks, and how much?

"Authorpreneur" takes a look at what's involved in independent publishing and what you can expect at different career phases.

About the Author

Kristen James is an outdoorsy girl who loves hiking, picking wild berries and mushrooms, and spending time with her family. Of course she loves reading and writing too! She discovered writing in the fourth grade when her class wrote short stories. Now she writes love stories with a twist of mystery and suspense set in the rugged and beautiful Pacific Northwest

James has over thirty published works which have hit the top 100 in Kindle in the US, UK, and Canada. Her fiction includes *Point Hope, More Than Memories,* and *All In My Head*. Learn more at www.writerkristenjames.com.